Pres

Carsyn

by

Anna and Will

on

May 11, 2003

My First Picture BIBLE STORIES

Kenneth N. Taylor

Illustrations by Nadine Wickenden
and Diana Catchpole

Our Sunday Visitor
Huntington, Indiana

To Parents:

You probably know the stories in this little book by heart. They are the timeless tales of heroism and heartache, courage and caring, struggles and success we call the Bible. Individually they are gripping stories; together they make up the foundation of our Faith.

When our children are still too little to know about the sacraments or to appreciate the mystery of the Mass, they can still be moved by the stories of Adam and Eve, David and Goliath, Daniel in the Lion's Den, Noah and the Ark, The Prodigal Son.

As parents, we have the privilege—and the responsibility—of passing on these stories to our children. Through these stories, the youngest members of our families can begin to know and love God.

I would urge you to not only take time to read and reread these stories to your children but to let them take this book with them—to church, to the grocery store, to the babysitter. By keeping these stories close at hand, you can help put the indelible imprint of Faith into the hearts and minds of your little ones.

Woodeene Koenig-Bricker
Editor, *Catholic Parent*

Here are a few ideas for using your Bible...

* Read or ask someone else to read you a different story each night before bed.
* Talk about the pictures, what happened in the story, and answer the question on each page.
* Use your Bible at dinnertime when your family is all together and read a story to begin the mealtime prayer.
* Take your Bible when you go somewhere in the car or anytime when you or someone else might have a few minutes to share an adventure.

Published in the United States by
Tyndale House Publishers, Inc.
351 Executive Drive
Carol Stream, Illinois 60188

ISBN 0-87973-108-7
ISBN 0-87973-109-5 (handled edition)

Dear Little Friend,

What is God like? What does God think about? What does God want me to do? These are just a few of the questions you may have about God. You will be able to tell a lot about God and God's Son, Jesus, from reading the Bible.

God has always made Himself known to us in a special way through the Bible. The Bible is full of amazing stories that help us know God better. Most importantly, we learn about God's great love for each one of us. In the Bible, John 3:16 says, "God is a God of love." This will become easy for you to understand as you read the Bible.

You will learn about: Creation, the first Christmas, stories Jesus told, miracles, friends of God, people Jesus loved and cared for, and much, much more!

We are praying that this Bible will open your heart and life to God's Good News for you! There is nothing that will make you happier than knowing and loving God.

Beth McNamara
Editor, *Christian Beginnings*

In the beginning was only God.
God made the whole world.

God made water and sky.
He made flowers and trees.
He put the sun in the sky.
He made fish and birds.

Everything was good.

GENESIS 1

Name something God made.

Next God made people. First he made a man named Adam.

God put Adam in a pretty garden called the Garden of Eden.

He told Adam to give names to all the animals. Then God made the first woman, Eve. She became Adam's wife.

They were very happy.

GENESIS 1-2

What job did God give Adam?

Adam and Eve did not obey God. So God made them leave the pretty garden.

What a sad day that was!

Adam and Eve could never go back to the Garden of Eden.

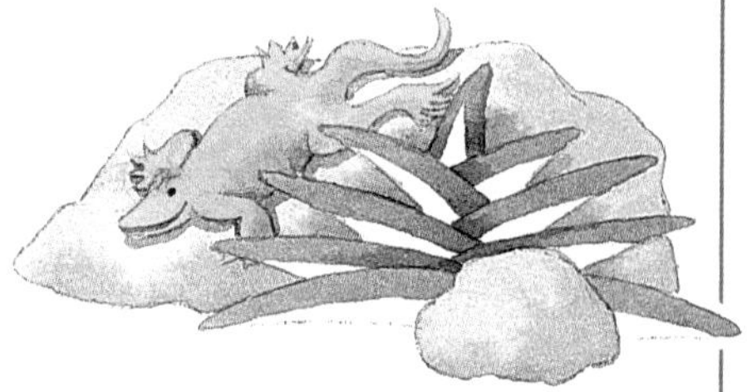

Angels with a flaming sword kept them away.

GENESIS 3

Why did Adam and Eve leave the garden?

Cain and Abel were brothers. Their parents were Adam and Eve.

Abel loved and obeyed God, but Cain did not. He was angry and killed Abel. This was very wrong, and God was very sad. The rest of Cain's life was hard and difficult.

GENESIS 4

How did God feel when Cain didn't obey him?

God said he would make it rain until there was water everywhere!

Noah believed God.

God told Noah to build a big boat. It was called an ark.

Noah obeyed God. Noah's three sons helped him build the boat on dry land.

God promised to keep Noah and his family safe and dry.

GENESIS 6

What was Noah's big boat called?

Finally the big boat was ready.

Then God said, "Noah, take two of each kind of animal and bird with you."

Everyone went into the ark. Then God shut the door.

GENESIS 7

Why did God want the animals and birds to go into the boat?

Noah and his family were safe inside the ark.

Then it began to rain.

It rained and rained.
Water covered the
whole earth. But
inside the ark,
it was dry.

GENESIS 7

Where was it safe and dry?

What is all that beautiful color in the sky? It's a rainbow! God put it there so he would remember his promise to never again cover the world with water.

Noah and his family and the animals came out of the ark. Then Noah thanked God for keeping them safe.

GENESIS 8-9

Why did God put a rainbow in the sky?

Some people tried to build a tower up to the sky. They wanted to show how great they were.

God was not happy, so he stopped them. He made them speak different languages. They couldn't understand each other! And they couldn't work together to finish the tower.

GENESIS 11

Why did the people want to build the tower?

Abraham was God's special friend.

God told Abraham and his wife, Sarah, to move to another country. God promised to do good things for them. Abraham obeyed God.

He knew God would help him, and he was not afraid. GENESIS 12

Why wasn't Abraham afraid?

Abraham and his nephew Lot lived near each other. They each owned many cows and sheep.

There wasn't enough grass for all the animals to eat. Abraham told Lot, "We must live in different places."

Because Lot was selfish, he chose the place with the most grass and water for himself.

GENESIS 13

Is it better to fight or to share?

Sarah and Abraham were sad.
They didn't have any children.

A long time ago God had promised them a son. Finally, when they were very old, their baby, Isaac, was born. Then Abraham and Sarah were very happy!

GENESIS 21

Is it easy for you to wait for things you want?

Isaac grew up
and married
Rebekah. They
had twin sons.

When their son Jacob grew up,
he left home one day. He slept
outside with his head on a rock!

Jacob
dreamed about
angels going up and down
steps from heaven. God said,
"I will be with you and
take care of you."

GENESIS 28

What did God tell Jacob in his dream?

Jacob and his twin brother, Esau, played together as boys.

When they grew up, Jacob played a mean trick on his brother.

That's when Jacob had to move far away.

Many years later, Jacob told Esau he wanted to be friends again. Esau ran to meet Jacob, and they hugged each other!

GENESIS 33

Did Jacob and Esau become friends again?

Jacob had twelve sons. One was Joseph.

Jacob loved
Joseph so much that he gave
him a special gift. It was a beautiful coat.

Jacob's other sons wanted beautiful coats too. They became angry with Joseph, and they were mean to him. GENESIS 37

Why were Joseph's brothers angry with him?

Baby Moses was not safe.
So his family hid him
in a basket.

A princess found the baby
floating in his basket.

Bad men wanted
to kill the baby.

God sent the princess
to find baby Moses
and take care of him.

EXODUS 2

Who kept baby Moses safe?

When Moses grew up, he took care of sheep.

One day he saw a bush on fire, but the bush didn't burn up! God talked to Moses from the bush. He said, "Lead my people out of Egypt." Moses didn't think he could do it, but God promised to help him.

EXODUS 3

What can God help you do?

God's people had to make bricks in Egypt.

Pharaoh, the king of Egypt, was very mean. He told his soldiers to whip God's people and make them work even harder. God sent Moses to tell Pharaoh to stop hurting the people.

EXODUS 5

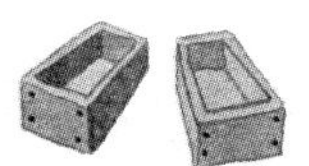

Moses helped people.
How can you help someone?

Moses asked Pharaoh to let God's people move to another country. But Pharaoh said no.

God punished Pharaoh by sending frogs and flies into every Egyptian home.

Pharaoh still wouldn't let God's people go. So God said the oldest son of each Egyptian family would die.

EXODUS 7-11

Why did God punish Pharaoh?

Pharaoh still wouldn't listen, so God punished him. But God kept his people safe. Everyone lived who sprinkled lamb's blood on their doors.

The night God did this is called the Passover.

Pharaoh finally told Moses to take God's people away. They left Egypt that very night!

EXODUS 12

How does God keep your family safe?

God's people followed Moses to the Red Sea. They didn't know how to get across it. God told Moses to hold up his stick.

When he did, God made a path through the water so the people could walk across on dry ground. They were safe!

EXODUS 14

How did God help his people?

God's people could not find any food.

They were very hungry.
God sent them little pieces
of bread from heaven.

Every morning he sent enough for that day.

EXODUS 16

What does God give you to eat?

God's people came to a place where there was no water to drink.

Moses asked God what to do for his thirsty people.

God told him to hit a big rock with his stick. When Moses did, water came out, and there was enough for everyone!

EXODUS 17

Remember to thank God for water to drink!

An army came to fight God's people.

As long as Moses raised his special stick toward heaven, God's people would win. But his arms got tired. So Moses' brother and a friend helped him.

They found a stone for him to sit on. They held his arms up until the sun went down. And God's people won the battle.

EXODUS 17

How can you help a brother, a sister, or a friend?

Moses climbed up a big mountain. There God gave him ten special rules on two stones. God wanted his people to know how to obey him.

One rule is to love God. Another rule is to love and obey your parents. We call these the Ten Commandments.

EXODUS 20, 24

What are God's rules called?

While Moses was on the mountain with God, Aaron made a calf. He made it from the gold jewelry everyone brought him.

The people worshiped the calf as if it were a god that could lead them.

This made God angry. But Moses asked God to forgive them. And God did.

EXODUS 32

Why was God angry with the people?

Moses gave the people God's directions for making a tabernacle. This was a special tent where God's people could worship him. Everyone worked hard until it was finished.

EXODUS 35-36

Where do you worship God?

The people moved to new places many times in the wilderness.

They moved on whenever a special cloud above the tabernacle moved.

God was in the cloud, and the people followed him.

EXODUS 40

God is with you, too. Thank him!

Moses sent twelve men to see the land God promised to give his people.

Joshua and Caleb came back to tell everyone what a beautiful country it was. The other ten men were scared of the giants who lived there. But Joshua and Caleb knew God would take care of them no matter what.

NUMBERS 13-14

When you're afraid, what can you do?

God's people were afraid. Poisonous snakes were biting some of them.

God told Moses to make a metal snake and put it on top of a pole. People with snakebites could look at the metal snake. Then God would heal them.

NUMBERS 21

When you are sick, who can make you well?

Balaam was taking a trip. God sent an angel with a sword to stop him. Balaam's donkey saw the angel and wouldn't move.

This made Balaam angry, and he hit his donkey.

Then the donkey talked! "What have I done?" he asked.

Finally Balaam saw the angel and listened to his message from God.

What did the donkey see first?

NUMBERS 22

After Moses died, God made Joshua the new leader. He had to help God's people cross the Jordan River.

Joshua told the men who carried the special box with God's laws inside to go first.

When they stepped into the river, the water flowed away. Then everyone could walk to the other side!

JOSHUA 3

How did Joshua help the people?

Joshua was the new leader of God's people. Their enemies would not let them into the city of Jericho. But God showed Joshua a way.

Joshua and the people marched around the walls of the city. They blew their horns and shouted.

Then the
big walls fell down!
God's people went inside.

JOSHUA 6

How did Joshua get inside the city?

Five armies came to fight Joshua and God's people.

Joshua's army was winning. But they needed more time. So Joshua prayed, "Let the sun stand still."

And God stopped the sun right in the middle of the sky! It didn't go down for a long time.

God's people won the battle.

JOSHUA 10

Do you think God can do anything?

Thousands of men were waiting to fight the enemies of God's people. God told Gideon that his army should be small.

Gideon took all the men to the river. God said only the 300 men who drank from their hands could be in the army.

Bravely Gideon took only these men, and God helped them win the fight! JUDGES 7

Will you let God help you be brave?

God made Samson
very, very strong.

He broke the ropes that tied him!

He killed a lion with his bare hands.

He knocked down a large building. It fell on many of God's enemies.

JUDGES 14-16

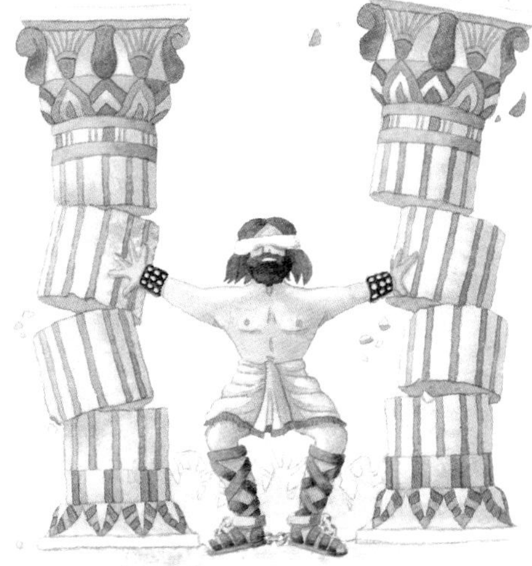

Who made Samson strong?

Job was a good man. He loved God, and God loved him.

But God let him become very sick.

He hurt all over.

But Job still loved God, even while he was sick.

JOB 1

Did Job stop loving God?

Naomi was very sad because her husband and two sons had died.

Ruth went with Naomi on a long trip to help her. Then God blessed both of them. God was pleased because Ruth was kind to Naomi.

RUTH 1

Name something kind you can do for someone in your family.

Samuel was Eli's helper.

One night when Samuel was sleeping, God called to him. "Samuel! Samuel!" The boy thought Eli was calling him.

Finally Samuel knew God was calling him. Samuel answered, “Tell me what you want, and I will do it.” 1 SAMUEL 2

Who was calling Samuel?

God chose Saul to be the king of God's people.
Saul was strong and good-looking.
But he didn't love God.
Saul did things that were wrong.

So God said he couldn't
be king anymore. 1 SAMUEL 8

Is it more important to be
strong or to love God?

David took care of his father's sheep.

He led them to
the best grass for the sheep to eat.

And David kept the sheep safe from wild animals like lions and bears. David was a good shepherd.

1 SAMUEL 16

What made David a good shepherd?

One day a lion tried to catch one of David's sheep and eat it. David grabbed the sheep away from the lion.

Then the lion tried to eat David!

But God helped David kill the lion. David was strong and brave.

1 SAMUEL 17

How did David keep his sheep safe?

Goliath was one of God's enemies. He was nine feet tall! He said he would kill anyone who dared to come and fight him.

David wasn't afraid of Goliath because he knew God was on his side.

David used his slingshot and a stone.

The stone hit Goliath between the eyes and killed him!

1 SAMUEL 17

Why wasn't David afraid?

After David killed Goliath, everyone praised him for being so brave.

One of his new friends was Jonathan, the king's son. Jonathan liked David so much that he gave him his robe and his sword. David and Jonathan were best friends.

1 SAMUEL 18

Do you have a best friend?

King Saul wanted to kill David.

One day the king and his soldiers looked for David, but they couldn't find him.

That night, while the king was sleeping, David came and took his spear. But David didn't hurt him, because God had chosen Saul to be king.

1 SAMUEL 26

Why didn't David hurt the king?

One day when David was taking care of his father's sheep, Samuel sent for him. When David came, he saw his father and brothers.

Samuel was talking to them. Samuel said that God wanted David to be the new king!

What a surprise to David and his family!

1 SAMUEL 16

What was Samuel's surprising news?

King Saul was killed in battle.
Then David became the new king.

He wanted the box with God's rules inside to be near him. So some men carried the special box into the city of Jerusalem. As they did, David and all the people celebrated with lots of singing and dancing.

2 SAMUEL 6

Do you have a Bible?
Then God's rules are near you!

One day King David saw a beautiful young woman. She was taking a bath in a pool near his palace. David wanted her for himself, so he did a terrible thing.

David told his men to kill her husband. God was angry and punished David for doing this.

But God never stopped loving him.

2 SAMUEL 11-12

When you do something wrong, does God still love you?

Absalom wanted to be king instead of his father, King David. One day Absalom was riding his donkey.

But his hair got caught in some tree branches.

His donkey walked away and left Absalom hanging from the tree. That's where David's soldiers found him!

2 SAMUEL 18

Why was Absalom hanging?

Solomon was King David's son. He rode on the king's mule.

David told him to do this so people would know that Solomon was their new king. One of God's helpers poured oil on Solomon's head to show that God was pleased. Many people played happy music. They prayed that King Solomon would live for a long time.

1 KINGS 1

Why did Solomon ride on King David's mule?

Solomon asked God to help him be a good king. So God made him very wise.

One day two women came to the king. Each of them wanted the same baby. Solomon was wise.

He said that the one who loved the baby could have him. Solomon knew that this woman was the baby's mother.

1 KINGS 3

What does it mean to be wise? Who can make you wise?

King Solomon built a temple. It was a beautiful building where people worshiped God.

Solomon talked to God there. He thanked God and praised him because God is so great and good.

Solomon asked God to always listen to his prayers and answer them.

1 KINGS 6, 8

Where do you worship God?
What do you say to him?

Solomon was a good king as long as he obeyed God. But Solomon began praying to animals made of gold and silver and even stone!

Could these fake gods answer his prayers? Of course not. Our real God was angry because Solomon did this. He said he would give Solomon's kingdom to somebody else.

1 KINGS 11

Why was God angry with Solomon?

Elijah was God's helper. Elijah told the king it would not rain for a long time because of the bad things the king was doing.

God wanted Elijah to be safe. He told him where he could go to hide from the king. Elijah would find water to drink there.

God had birds bring him food in their beaks.

1 KINGS 17

Can you trust God to give you food and water?

Elijah wanted everyone to know that God answers prayer.

So he asked some people to pour out a lot of water on some wood and stones. Then Elijah asked God to send fire from heaven.

Water always puts out fires. But the fire that God sent burned up the water!

1 KINGS 18

Tell about a time when God answered one of your prayers.

God wanted Elijah to live with him in heaven forever. So God sent horses made of fire to bring Elijah to him.

They were pulling a wagon called a chariot. It was made of fire, too. Elijah rode in the chariot all the way up to heaven!

Elisha, who was God's new helper, watched him go.

2 KINGS 2

You know someone who is in heaven.

His name is Jesus!

A woman with two sons had no money, but she had a jar of cooking oil.

Elisha said, "Get a lot of empty jars from your friends. Fill the jars with oil from your jar."

The woman poured and poured the oil from her jar. But no matter how much oil she poured, God kept her jar full of oil!

Elisha told the woman to sell the oil so she would have plenty of money.

2 KINGS 4

It was God who showed Elisha how to help. Who can help your family?

Elisha often walked from town to town so he could be God's helper in different places.

A man and woman in one town always let him stay at their house. One day their son died. But when Elisha prayed, God made the boy come back to life!

2 KINGS 4

Is there anything that God can't do?

Naaman was the king's most important soldier. But he had bad sores on his skin A young girl said that Elisha, God's helper, could make Naaman get well.

So Naaman rode in his chariot to the country where Elisha lived.

Elisha told Naaman to wash in the Jordan River seven times. As soon as he did it, God healed him!

2 KINGS 5

Tell about a time when you were sick and God showed a doctor how to help you.

King Joash wanted God's house to be beautiful.

The people brought their money to God's house.

The money was used to buy wood and stones.

And it was used to pay the workers who made God's house beautiful again.

2 KINGS 12

Will you give some of your money to God?

God told Jonah to go to Nineveh. But he went on a boat to another city. Then God sent a storm.

Jonah was thrown overboard. A huge fish swallowed him.

After three days the fish coughed him out. Then Jonah went where God told him to go.

JONAH 1-2

Thank God for helping you do the things he wants you to do.

Hezekiah was a very good king.
He always obeyed God.
Other kings had worshiped big
gold idols that looked like
people or animals.

King Hezekiah and his helpers
smashed the idols. The king knew
that these were just fake gods.

2 KINGS 18

What made Hezekiah a good king?

King Josiah wanted to do what was right. But he didn't know God's rules. They had been lost for a long time.

When the rules were found, someone read them to Josiah.

The king was sorry that he had not been obeying God's rules. So he asked God to forgive him. And God did.

2 KINGS 22

How can you know the right thing to do?

Jeremiah gave people messages from God. The people did not want to listen to Jeremiah.

Some men threw him into a deep hole so he couldn't give more of God's messages.

But the king told his men to get Jeremiah out.

JEREMIAH 38

How did God take care of Jeremiah?

Daniel and his three friends were living in a country far away from their homes.

They loved God and always wanted to obey him. So God made them wise.

They gave good advice to the king. They could always tell him the best thing to do.

DANIEL 1

Who can make you wise?

The king ordered his people to make a giant statue that looked like him. He said everyone had to bow down and worship it.

Daniel's three friends wouldn't do it. They said they would worship only God, no matter what the king would do to them.

DANIEL 3

Why wouldn't Daniel's friends do what the king said?

The king heard that Shadrach, Meshach, and Abednego would not worship his gold statue.

So he gave orders to throw them into a very hot fire.

Then the king saw someone else in the fire. It was an angel, sent by God to keep the three men safe!

DANIEL 3

Why weren't the men hurt in the fire?

One night the king was giving a big party. Suddenly everyone saw a hand writing some words on the wall.

The king was afraid. He asked Daniel what the words meant. Daniel said it was a message from God, telling him he could no longer be king.

DANIEL 5

Why was the king afraid?

Daniel loved praying to God. But the king said, "Don't pray to God. Pray to me instead!" Daniel knew this was wrong, so he kept praying only to God.

The king's men threw Daniel into a den of hungry lions.

But God sent an angel. The angel kept the lions from hurting Daniel.

DANIEL 6

Why didn't the lions hurt Daniel?

Esther was a beautiful queen. She was Jewish, but the king didn't know that. He signed a law for all Jewish people to be killed.

Queen Esther was afraid, but she was brave. She asked the king to save her people. So the king signed a new law to help the Jews.

ESTHER 5-8

Why did the king decide to help the Jewish people?

God's people built a beautiful building where they could worship him.

The people worked hard because they wanted to please God. They wanted to have a special place to pray.

God is happy when we pray and worship him.

EZRA 6

Do you remember to pray?

God's people worked hard to build up the wall around Jerusalem.

They thanked God for helping them. Some of the people marched right on top of the wall, praising God as they marched.

What a happy day it was! The people were excited that God kept their enemies away.

NEHEMIAH 3, 12

Can you march and sing thank-you songs to God?

God sent the angel Gabriel to tell Mary something very important.

At first Mary was afraid. But the angel said, "God wants you to be the mother of his Son, Jesus!" Mary said she would do whatever God wanted. She was very happy to become Jesus' mother.

LUKE 1

Will you do whatever God wants you to do?

Zechariah and Elizabeth were very old when they had a baby boy.

Zechariah knew he would call the baby John because that's what an angel told him to do.

God helped Zechariah know that his son would tell many people about Jesus when he grew up.

LUKE 1

What can you tell people about Jesus?

Mary and Joseph came to the town of Bethlehem.

The inn was full, so they stayed in a stable with the animals. God's Son was born that night. Mary named her baby Jesus.

LUKE 2

Sing a song to Jesus!

On the night Jesus was born, some shepherds were taking care of their sheep. An angel came to tell them that they could find baby Jesus in a manger.

Suddenly thousands of angels appeared in the sky.

They praised God for sending Jesus to be our Savior.

LUKE 2

You can thank God for Jesus too!

When the angels left, the shepherds said, "Let's go to Bethlehem. Let's see if we can find this baby."

They found Jesus lying in a manger, just as the angel had said. How excited they were! They told everyone the good news. They praised God all the way back to their fields.

LUKE 2

You can tell everyone about Jesus' birth too!

Simeon was an old man. Before he died, he wanted to see God's Son.

One day God told Simeon that he should go to the temple. Simeon saw baby Jesus there!

Simeon held God's little Son in his arms and thanked God for him.

LUKE 2

Whose Son is Jesus?

Some wise men followed a special star in the sky. It led them to the house where the little boy Jesus lived.

The wise men gave gifts to Jesus. They got down on their knees to worship him. They knew he was going to be a great king.

MATTHEW 2

You can give Jesus a gift too. Tell him you love him!

An angel told Joseph that Jesus wasn't safe in Bethlehem. Egypt was a safe place for Jesus.

So Joseph, Mary, and Jesus left for Egypt while it was still dark.

Joseph was glad that he could take good care of God's Son.

MATTHEW 2

Who *takes care of you*?

God sent an angel to Joseph. The angel told him it was safe to take Jesus home.

Joseph took his family out of Egypt. They went to live in the town of Nazareth. Jesus became a strong and wise boy. He loved his parents, and they loved him.

MATTHEW 2, LUKE 2

Ask God to help you grow strong and wise.

Jesus went to the temple with his family when he was twelve.

The teachers were surprised at how much Jesus knew about God.

They didn't know that Jesus was God's Son. No wonder he knew so much about God!

LUKE 2

Where can you learn more about God?

John the Baptist was Jesus' cousin.

When Jesus grew up, he asked John to baptize him in the Jordan River.

Then the Holy Spirit came down from heaven as a beautiful dove.

And God said to Jesus, "You are my dear Son. I am very pleased with you."

LUKE 3

What did God tell Jesus?

A man named Nicodemus came to talk to Jesus one night.

Jesus told Nicodemus that God loved everyone so much that he even sent his Son to die for us. Now everyone who believes in Jesus, God's Son, can go to heaven someday.

JOHN 3

How did God show his love for us?

Jesus chose twelve men to be his disciples.
They went with him everywhere.
They saw him do many miracles,
like making blind people see.

He taught them about God. And he told them about heaven, where he lived before he came to earth. He was their friend. You can be Jesus' friend too.

JOHN 1

Would you like to be Jesus' friend?

Jesus was tired and thirsty from a long walk. So he asked a woman for some water.

He told her he could give her the kind of joy that lasts forever. He told her that God sent him. The woman believed this and told everyone about Jesus.

JOHN 4

Do you love Jesus?
Then your joy will last forever too!

Jesus got into a boat with some fishermen. They had been fishing all night without catching anything.

Jesus told them to try again.

The men listened to Jesus, and they caught more fish than their nets could hold! The fishermen were very surprised. They decided to follow Jesus.

LUKE 5

Why did the fishermen follow Jesus?

Jesus was teaching a large crowd. Four men wanted Jesus to help a friend who couldn't walk.

So they lowered him through the roof.

They set him down in front of Jesus.

First Jesus forgave the man's sins. Then he told the man to get up and walk, and he did!

Everyone thanked God!

LUKE 5

What did Jesus do for the man who couldn't walk?

Another man had been sick for a long time. Jesus asked him if he would like to get well.

The man said, "Yes!" So Jesus told him, "Stand up and walk." Suddenly the man was able to get up and walk!

JOHN 5

How did the man get well?

One day Jesus sat down on the side of a mountain.

A large crowd of people came to hear him talk about God. He taught them how to love God and live for him.

Jesus said this was the way to have a happy life.

MATTHEW 5

How can you have a happy life?

A Roman soldier asked Jesus to heal his servant, who was very sick.

Jesus said he would come to the soldier's house. But the soldier believed that Jesus could stay where he was and just say "Be healed."

So Jesus did. And the servant got well as soon as Jesus said this!

MATTHEW 8

What did the soldier believe Jesus could do?

The father of a very sick little girl begged Jesus to make his daughter well again.

On the way to her house, Jesus heard that the little girl had died.

Jesus went to her house anyway. He said, "Get up, my child!" The little girl stood up. She was alive and well again!

LUKE 8

What did Jesus do for a little girl who died?

This man was blind.
He couldn't see anything.

His friends brought him to Jesus. They asked Jesus to touch the man and heal him. Jesus put his hands on the man's eyes. Suddenly he could see everything clearly!

MARK 8

What did the blind man's friends do for him?

Look at the big waves!

The disciples' small boat
was about to sink. Jesus was quietly sleeping in the boat. "Wake up!" his disciples yelled. They were afraid.

Jesus got up and told the storm to stop. Then the waves became calm and quiet. Jesus could do wonderful things like that.

LUKE 8

What did Jesus tell the storm to do?

Did you ever try to walk on water? Of course not! But Jesus did.

One night the disciples were crossing the lake in their boat. Suddenly they saw Jesus walking toward them on the water.

They screamed in terror! But Jesus told them who it was. He told them not to be afraid.

MATTHEW 14

Why were the disciples afraid?

Jesus took Peter, James and John to the top of a high hill.

Suddenly Jesus' face began to shine, and his clothes became as white as snow.

Then they saw Jesus talking to Moses and Elijah, who lived long ago.

And a voice from a bright cloud said, "Jesus is my much loved Son. Listen to him."

MATTHEW 17

What did the voice from heaven say?

A big crowd of people followed Jesus. When they got hungry there were no stores to buy food.

A boy gave his lunch of five pieces of bread and two fish to Jesus.

Then Jesus made the bread and fish
become thousands of pieces.
Everybody had enough to eat.
There were even leftovers!

JOHN 6

The boy gave his lunch to Jesus.
Can you think of something you can give Jesus?

A woman whose husband died had only two pennies. Instead of buying something to eat, she put them in the church collection box.

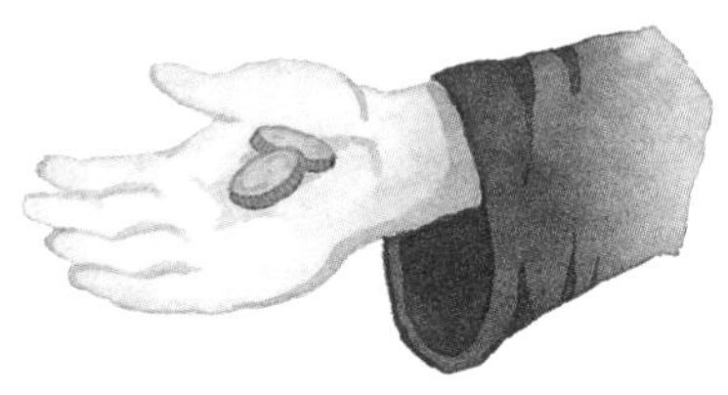

She did this because she loved God. Jesus said she gave more than the rich men who put in many dollars. She put in all she had. But the rich men gave God only a tiny part of their money.

LUKE 21

What can you give God to show him you love him?

Some mothers brought their little children to Jesus. They wanted him to touch and bless them. Jesus' disciples told the mothers not to bother Jesus.

But Jesus loved children. He called them to come to him. Jesus said children can believe in him and love him even when they are little.

LUKE 18

Do you love Jesus?

This man was hurt by men who stole his money. They left him in the ditch half dead.

A man he didn't like saw him there. This man put bandages on his cuts. Then he put the man on his donkey and took him to town.

He took care of him. We call the man who helped him the Good Samaritan.

LUKE 10

How can you help someone and be a Good Samaritan?

Jesus liked to visit two sisters, Mary and Martha.

Martha worked hard in the kitchen making dinner for Jesus. Mary just wanted to talk with him and learn more about God. Martha scolded Mary for not helping her.

But Jesus said Mary was doing the right thing by listening to him. We listen to Jesus when we read the Bible.

LUKE 10

How can you listen to Jesus?

A shepherd takes good care
of his sheep night and day.

Jesus said we are his sheep.
And he cares for us all the time.
He is the Good Shepherd who
knows the names of all his sheep.
You are a little lamb and Jesus
knows your name.

JOHN 10

Why is Jesus a good shepherd?

Mary and Martha had a brother named Lazarus. Lazarus got sick and died.

His sisters knew that Jesus could have healed him. And now it was too late. Lazarus was dead.

But Jesus went to Lazarus' grave and called, "Lazarus, come out." And Lazarus came out of the grave, alive again!

JOHN 11

How did Jesus help Lazarus?

Ten men with bad sores asked Jesus to make them well.

Jesus told them to go and show their pastor that the sores had gone away.

As they went, they suddenly got well again!

But only one man came back to thank Jesus. Jesus wondered why the other men didn't thank him.

LUKE 17

What can you thank Jesus for today?

A man had two sons. The younger son asked his father for a lot of money.

Then the son moved far away. He did bad things. Soon he ran out of money. He went home to tell his father, "I was wrong." His father was waiting for him and ran to meet him. He gave his son a big hug!

LUKE 15

How did the father show his son that he still loved him?

People didn't like Zacchaeus. He cheated them out of their money. But Zacchaeus wanted to see Jesus.

He was too short to see over the crowd, so he climbed a tree.

When Jesus walked by, he looked up and told Zacchaeus, "I'm coming to your house."

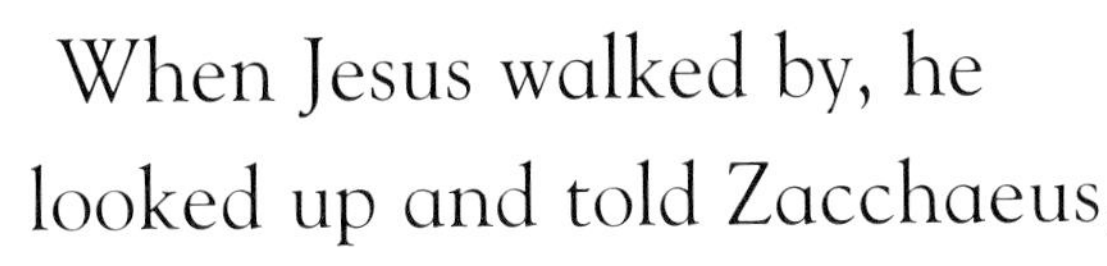

After Zacchaeus met Jesus, he stopped cheating people.

LUKE 19

What did Jesus tell Zacchaeus?

One day Jesus rode a donkey into Jerusalem.

Children sang about how wonderful Jesus was

Many people waved palm branches. They thanked God for Jesus. They wanted Jesus to be their new king. LUKE 19

Tell God how wonderful Jesus is!

Jesus is eating supper with his good friends for the last time. This is called the Last Supper.

Jesus gave them bread and wine and said, "This is my Body and Blood. Do this to remember me."

He knew soldiers soon would take him away and kill him. Jesus died for you and me.

LUKE 22

Why was this the last meal Jesus would eat with his disciples?

After supper Jesus took his disciples to a garden to pray. Jesus felt very sad.

He knew the soldiers were coming soon. He knelt down and prayed for God to help him. His disciples were no help—they all fell asleep! But God sent an angel to make Jesus strong and brave.

LUKE 22

Why did God send an angel to Jesus?

Judas was one of Jesus' disciples, but he only pretended to love Jesus. Some leaders gave Judas money to tell them where to find Jesus.

Judas led some soldiers to arrest Jesus.

The other disciples were afraid. They didn't help Jesus. They ran away.

LUKE 22

Why didn't the disciples help Jesus?

Peter was one of Jesus' disciples. He was afraid of the soldiers who took Jesus away. So he told three people, "I don't know Jesus!"

Later Peter was sorry he lied. Jesus forgave him. After that, Peter wanted to tell everyone about Jesus!

LUKE 22

How did Peter feel after he lied? What did Jesus do then?

The soldiers took Jesus to a judge named Pilate.

Pilate decided Jesus hadn't done anything wrong. He wanted to let him go. But the people kept yelling, "Kill him, Kill him!"

They shouted louder and louder until Pilate said the soldiers could do this terrible thing.

LUKE 23

Why didn't Pilate let Jesus go free?

The soldiers nailed Jesus to a cross made of wood. They put two bad men on crosses next to him.

One of the bad men was sorry for his sins. He asked Jesus to forgive him. Jesus said yes, he would do that.

Jesus forgives everyone
who asks him to.
He will forgive you.

LUKE 23

What must we do if we want Jesus to forgive us?

After Jesus was dead, some friends put his body in a cave.

A big stone was put in front of the cave so no one could go in or out.

But early on Sunday morning Jesus came back to life and came out of the grave! He was alive again!

LUKE 24

Did Jesus stay in the cave?

Jesus' friends could hardly believe that he was alive again. So he showed them the nail marks in his hands and feet.

One day he rose up into the sky and disappeared in a cloud! He went back to his Father in heaven. Someday he will come back to earth again!

LUKE 24, ACTS 1

Where did Jesus go?

After Jesus had gone to heaven, his friends had a big meeting. Suddenly there was a loud noise!

Little flames of fire sat on their heads, but the fire didn't burn them.

God's Holy Spirit came to live in their hearts. The Holy Spirit helps us believe in Jesus.

ACTS 2

Who came to live in the hearts of Jesus' friends?

Paul didn't believe that Jesus was God's son. He even tried to kill people who believed in Jesus.

One day a bright light blinded him, and he fell down.

Then he heard a voice.
It was Jesus!

After that Paul traveled many places just to tell people about Jesus.

ACTS 9

Whose voice did Paul hear?

Many people believed in Jesus when they heard Paul preach in Damascus.

But some people wanted to kill him. They watched for him at the city gate.

Paul's friends put him in a big basket. Then they lowered him to the ground through a hole in the wall. He was safe!

ACTS 9

How did Paul's friends help him?

A man named Cornelius wanted to know more about God.

So an angel told Cornelius where to find Peter.

Cornelius sent two of his servants to invite Peter to visit him.

Then Peter told Cornelius and his friends how Jesus could forgive their sins.

ACTS 10

What did Peter tell Cornelius?

"Stop telling people about Jesus!" the soldiers said to Peter. But Peter wouldn't stop.

So the soldiers put Peter in jail and chained him to two soldiers.

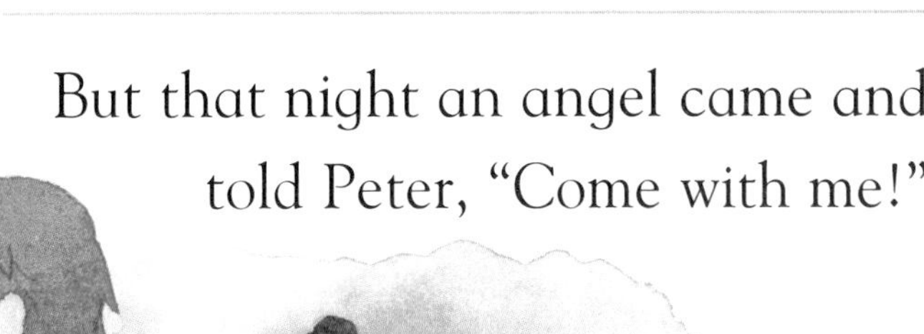

But that night an angel came and told Peter, "Come with me!"

Peter's chains fell off, and the prison doors opened. Peter was free!

ACTS 12

How did Peter get out of jail?

Timothy's mother and grandmother loved God.

They knew that Jesus loved them and died on the cross so that God could forgive their sins. They taught Timothy these things when he was very young, and he gave his life to Jesus. Timothy told God he would always obey him.

2 TIMOTHY 1

Who taught Timothy about Jesus?

Paul met with a group of women who were praying by the banks of a river.

He told them all about Jesus being God's Son.

One of the women was Lydia. She believed in God, but had never heard of Jesus.

After she listened to Paul, Lydia believed in Jesus, too.

ACTS 16

How did Lydia hear about Jesus?

Some people threw Paul and Silas into jail for preaching about Jesus. During the night the men sang to God.

Then God sent an earthquake. The prison doors flew open and the prisoners' chains flew off!

The jailer was afraid. Paul told him and his family about Jesus. Then they all believed in Jesus!

ACTS 16

What happened after the earthquake?

Paul met a husband and wife, Aquila and Priscilla.

They made tents for a living. Paul made tents too.

He taught them all about Jesus, God's Son. And they believed in Jesus.

Later Aquila and Priscilla went with Paul to another town to tell people there about Jesus.

ACTS 18

Why did Aquila and Priscilla go with Paul?

John had been one of Jesus' best friends. When John was very old, Jesus came to him in a vision. Jesus told John about things that will happen.

The best thing is this: Jesus will come back someday! Then everyone who believes in Jesus will live with him forever in heaven.

REVELATION 1

What was the best thing Jesus told John?

Kenneth N. Taylor is best known as the creator of *The Living Bible*, which has been revised by a group of biblical scholars to become the New Living Translation. Ken and his wife, Margaret, have ten grown children and 28 grandchildren, so he has personally told many children about God!

Kenneth Taylor continues to have a passion for sharing the gospel with children through his writing. Some of his recent books include *Right Choices*, *Everything a Child Should Know about God*, and *Family Devotions for Children.*

U.S. Creative Director Jim Bolton
U.S. Editors Claudia Volkman, Betty Free
U.S. Bible Editor Dave Barrett

Designers Peter Bailey, Ann Salisbury
Publishing Manager Sarah Phillips
Deputy Art Director Mark Richards